PHILIPPIANS STUDY GUIDE

PHILIPPIANS
STUDY GUIDE

Michael Owen

THE CHRISTADELPHIAN
404 SHAFTMOOR LANE
BIRMINGHAM B28 8SZ
ENGLAND

1988

First Published 1988

ISBN 0 85189 124 1

Printed and bound in Great Britain by
Ebenezer Baylis and Son Ltd., Worcester

CONTENTS

WHAT IS A STUDY GUIDE?

1. **Aims:** The over-riding aim of all Bible study is that through knowledge and understanding of the word of God a person may become "wise unto salvation through faith which is in Christ Jesus" (2 Timothy 3:15).

"Study Guides" will plan special emphasis on:
a) First Principles of Doctrine
b) Practical Outcomes

They should be helpful to young people, to those who are "young in the faith", who often have very little background knowledge of the Scriptures, and to those of all ages and experience who enjoy straightforward, uncomplicated study of the Bible.

2. **Other Features of Study Guides**

a) *Layout*: After a brief introduction to the book, the first study section ("A Closer Look") provides essential background information. "Finding Your Way" enables the reader to see an overall picture of the book. Thereafter the study is on a verse by verse basis. Headings and bold verse references make it easy to use the guide for looking up information on any section of the Bible text.

b) *Bible Versions*: The Authorised Version (A.V.) remains the most used translation in Christadelphian ecclesias today. It is important therefore that we are at ease with its language, in spite of the difficulties for newcomers. These guides use the A.V. as their basis, explaining the language as far as possible. Other good modern versions, such as the Revised Standard Version (R.S.V.), the Revised Authorised Version (R.A.V./N.K.J.V.), and the New International Version (N.I.V.) are referred to and are helpful for a preliminary read through the book being studied. Most popular modern versions are unreliable and betray the doctrinal bias of their translators.

c) *Manageable Sections:* Each Guide is divided into units of study which are not too long. This will make it easier for individuals or groups to make progress. An hour's concentrated and productive study on a regular basis in likely to yield good results.

d) *Visual Help:* The prophets and the Lord Jesus himself used visual illustrations to communicate their message. While the prime emphasis is on the written word, visual help is given wherever possible to increase understanding.

e) *Use Alongside Bible:* The student must have a Bible open alongside the Guide. It is recommended at the outset that important information is marked in the Bible. Have a pencil and rubber at the ready.

f) *Assessment of Progress:* At the end of each section you are invited to "Test Yourself". Some questions ask for factual recall, others for understanding, others are open-ended, challenging readers to relate the lessons learned to their own lives.

It is suggested that readers *write down* their responses before looking up the suggested answers supplied towards the end of the guide. The point is not to see how clever anyone is, but to ensure a good knowledge and understanding has been achieved before moving on.

g) *Further Study:* The final sections contain suggestions for further study and a book list chosen on the basis of sound expositional and doctrinal content.

h) *Prayer:* We are studying the Word of God. Before commencing any Bible study we must ask God's blessing on our activity. Thank God for making the Bible available to us, so that through it we may come to know Him and to look forward to His coming Kingdom.

Here is a prayer that sums up our aim:
"Open thou mine eyes,
    that I may behold
Wondrous things out of thy law."

(Psalm 119:18)

PREFACE

The Bible is a book many feel they would like to understand better. For it is a book which has wonderfully changed people's lives. It claims to be the word of God. In it we can learn all about the Lord Jesus Christ.

But some of it is difficult to read (and sometimes the language of the translations is hard to follow). Some find it difficult to set about study. This Study Guide is intended to help—at least as far as Paul's Letter to the Philippians is concerned. Those new to the Bible, those who have been reading it for many years but would like to know it better, those who find existing commentaries too hard to make headway with—this is for you!

Many study classes, Bible reading groups and youth circles may also appreciate the opportunity of working through a book of the Bible, with each member of the group making use of the Study Guide and tackling the assignments.

Like the periodical *Faith Alive!*, the Study Guide is presented in as lively a fashion as possible, and in particular I have tried to relate the text to practical problems of life. The Study Guide is divided into reasonably digestible sections, with questions for you to check your progress before moving on. At the end there are suggested assignments for further, deeper study.

My thanks to the many brethren and sisters who have listened to me talking about *Philippians*, including those in Perth, Western Australia, for whom I commenced this study. I hope at least *some* of your helpful comments have been incorporated into this small work. Thanks too to those who have laboured before, whose studies have been a source of great assistance.

It gives me particular pleasure that this Study Guide will first be made available to the young people attending the 1989 Australian Christadelphian Youth Conference in Queensland, with its theme "Rejoice in the Lord". May all who use it come to a full appreciation of Philippians and through it of God's saving message, that they too may "rejoice in the Lord".

MICHAEL OWEN
Sidmouth, Devon

August 1988

ACKNOWLEDGEMENTS

For assistance in the production of illustrations, cover graphics and maps, grateful thanks are extended to Gerald Newton and Paul Wasson.

2

INTRODUCTION

WHAT IS THE BOOK ABOUT?

Paul's letter to the Philippians is a wonderfully warm and encouraging piece of writing, reflecting the strong bond of affection which linked Paul and the believers in Philippi, a town in what is now northern Greece.

Inspired Writing

Paul was an apostle (= specially sent by Jesus) and his epistles (old word for letters) are part of the *inspired* writings of the Bible. This means he was not simply writing as a man—even though he had a brilliant mind and was an outstanding example of a believer in Christ. He wrote under the direction of the *Holy Spirit*, promised to the apostles by Jesus so that they could establish groups of believers on the basis of the true teaching of the Gospel (see John 14:26; Acts 2; 2 Timothy 3:16,17).

Living Faith

Through reading and understanding this letter we gain an insight into the living faith of believers in the First Century of the Christian era—those who were closest to the Lord Jesus Christ himself.

God is wanting people like us today to believe just as they believed. The Bible tells us He is going to send Jesus again to our world to change it completely to a world of right living, peace and happiness for all people. This is what the good news (or Gospel) of the Kingdom of God is all about. It is what Jesus came to make

possible. The whole of the Bible is designed to prepare us for it. *Philippians* plays its part in telling us how to be ready.

What do we Find in the Letter?

Philippi was the first *ecclesia* (body of believers) Paul established in Europe. After he had left Philippi to continue his missionary activity, he maintained contact with the ecclesia. Written when Paul had been arrested and imprisoned, the letter contains:

1. News about Paul's imprisonment, with encouragement from the apostle to the believers to hold fast to their faith in the face of opposition.

2. News about *Timothy*, who had become Paul's assistant, and about *Epaphroditus*, who was sent by the Philippians to cheer Paul in his trials.

3. Thanks for their gifts to support his preaching work.

4. Strong reminders of the need for unity in the ecclesia.

5. Warnings not to be influenced by the *Judaizers*, who wanted to push believers back into the practices of the Jewish religion.

6. Many passages setting out the lovely qualities of lives influenced by the teaching of the Bible, specially the *joy* which comes from faith in Christ.

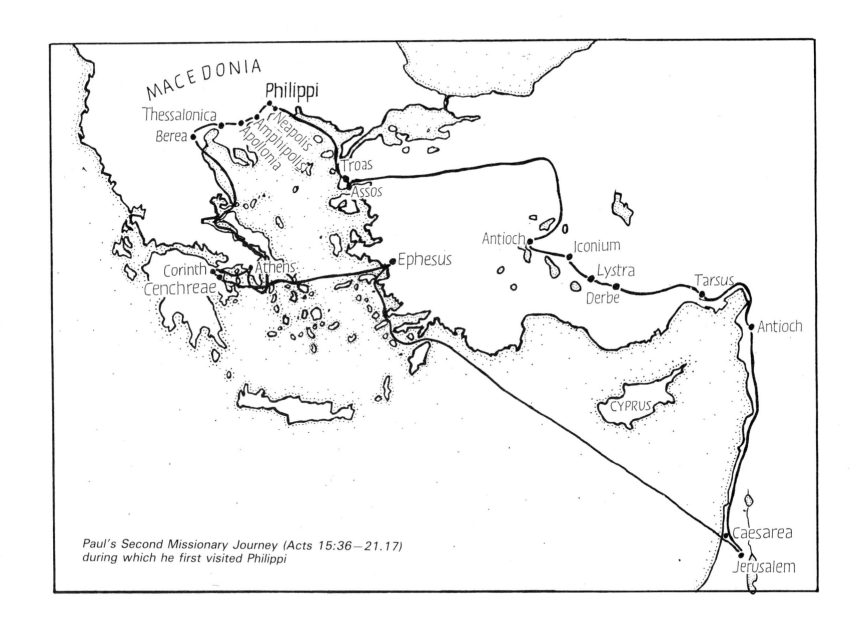

MACEDONIA

Philippi

Thessalonica
Berea
Neapolis
Amphipolis
Apollonia

Troas
Assos

Antioch
Iconium
Lystra
Derbe
Tarsus

Ephesus

Corinth
Cenchreae
Athens

Antioch

CYPRUS

Caesarea
Jerusalem

*Paul's Second Missionary Journey (Acts 15:36—21.17)
during which he first visited Philippi*

A CLOSER LOOK

THE ECCLESIA AT PHILIPPI

Where is Philippi?

Philippi was a *Roman Colony* founded by Philip of Macedon (the father of Alexander the Great). It was about 10 miles from the sea, in the province of *Macedonia*, right by the main road from Asia to Rome.

As a Roman colony its laws and administration were modelled on Rome's. It was a popular place for retired Roman soldiers to live and the citizens of Philippi were proud of their Roman status.

Why did Paul go there?

Paul was called out by the Lord "to bear my name before the *Gentiles* (those who are not Jews)" (Acts 9:15). It was part of the divine plan that the Gospel should spread from Jerusalem and Judea "unto the uttermost part of the earth" (Acts 1:8). Clearly Paul, with his Roman citizenship as well as his strict Jewish education, was an ideal choice to carry the Gospel message westwards.

During the *First Missionary Journey* Paul established a number of new ecclesias in Asia Minor (better known to us as Turkey). After reporting back to Antioch and Jerusalem he decided to "go again and visit our brethren in every city where we have preached the Word of the Lord, and see how they do (fare, R.V.)" (Acts 15:36). So the *Second Missionary Journey* got under way. The map shows the route.

Acts 16 informs us that Paul and his companions were guided by God not to preach at that time in Asia Minor, but to cross over the sea to Macedonia. This was clearly a momentous step for Paul, for now he was going to preach the Gospel in Europe for the first time.

Read Acts 16:6-10. Notice that in verse 10 the pronoun changes to "we". *Luke* was the writer of "Acts". He must have now joined *Paul, Silas and Timothy*. It has been suggested that Philippi was Luke's home town. This may have influenced the decision to go to Philippi first.

How was the ecclesia started?

The rest of Acts 16 (verses 11-40) tells us about the first converts in Philippi and the founding of the ecclesia. ***Read*** through this section of Acts.

Notice in particular the following:

1. The references to the *Roman Colony* (v. 12), with its magistrates and other Roman-style officials (vv. 20-22; 35-36). The people are proud of being Romans (v. 21) and intensely embarrassed when they discover that Paul and his friends are Roman citizens who should not have been treated so roughly (vv. 37-38).

2. The *Hardship* which Paul and Silas endured for the sake of the Gospel. The slave girl who told fortunes had some kind of mental problem which Paul cured. Her owners were so annoyed that they brought serious charges against Paul and Silas which led to a nasty beating and

imprisonment. "The inner prison" was no doubt dark, damp and foul. But the faithful companions knew how to rejoice in suffering, drawing personal strength from their recollection of the way Christ had "endured the cross and despised the shame".

3. The process of *conversion*. In each case there was careful *instruction* which led up to baptism.

Lydia was a business woman who already "worshipped God", because she was a Jewess or, more probably, a convert to the Jewish faith. She had a reasonable amount of knowledge on which the Apostle could build, with God's help. Unless we let God open our hearts and minds ("heart" here means both) by submitting to His Word willingly, we cannot be taught. Lydia was a prayerful person who wanted to know the Truth. So "she attended unto the things which were spoken of Paul" (v. 14). As a result of *faith* in what had been learnt, both she "and her household" were baptized.

The *Jailor* was clearly impressed by the wonderful spirit shown by Paul and Silas during their beating and imprisonment. He listened to their prayers and hymn singing and was so amazed by their refusal to take advantage of the earthquake to escape from prison, that he fell down before them and said, "Sirs, what must I do to be saved?" What he had already heard had taught him of the need to be saved! Paul now told him that he had to "believe on the Lord Jesus Christ". But it was not sufficient just to repeat this phrase on the basis of emotion and ignorance. He needed to *understand* what was the basis of this belief. So Paul and

Silas "spake unto him the word of the Lord, and to all that were in his house" (v. 32).

Once again conversion was not instantaneous and in ignorance. It involved *knowledge* and *understanding* of the Gospel of the Kingdom of God and was followed by *baptism*.

Understanding Baptism

We can now understand better the description of baptism as "the answer of a good conscience towards God" (1 Peter 3:21). Jesus himself was baptized and said, "Thus it becometh us (is fitting for us) to fulfil all righteousness" (Matthew 3:15). "He that believeth and is baptized shall be saved" (Mark 16:16). Baptism can only be real when a person knows about the Gospel and believes that by accepting the gift of salvation in Jesus Christ there is forgiveness of sins and the hope of eternal life in the Kingdom of God.

Baptism is both a birth and a death. When a person is completely "buried" in water it is a symbol of being buried with Christ. By his death, Jesus destroyed the power of sin, and, by his resurrection, he broke the power of death. When the person comes up out of the water, a new life commences. It is like a new birth, into the family of God. The new life is now linked to the life of the risen Lord Jesus. At the second coming of Jesus, God promises to give eternal life to faithful members of His family (Look up John 3:5; Acts 8:35-38; Romans 6:3-9).

WILLING SPIRIT
▼
PRAYER
▼
LEARN FROM THE WORD OF GOD
▼
INSTRUCTION FROM THE WISE
▼
FAITH
▼
LEADS TO DESIRE TO BECOME MEMBER OF GOD'S FAMILY BY BAPTISM

The Process of Conversion

How was the ecclesia kept going?

A small group of believers had been established. But it was necessary for Paul to continue along the great Roman road to the west. He realised that these new brethren and sisters ought to be helped to "continue steadfastly in the apostles' doctrine and fellowship, in breaking of bread, and in prayers" (Acts 2:42). This emphasises that baptism is only a beginning. It is a new birth. No baby with loving parents is left to fend for itself. New converts need help. They must be fed— their knowledge of God's Word must be built up. They must be kept warm and loved. Plenty of contact must strengthen fellowship.

It seems almost certain that Luke, whose home town was probably Philippi, was assigned the job of following up the Philippi campaign when Paul and his companions continued their journeys. Notice the pronoun "we" introduced in Acts 16:10 is dropped in Acts 17:1. It is re-introduced in chapter 20:6 when, on the *Third Missionary Journey*, Luke rejoins Paul and company as they travel through Philippi! This is a marvellous example of the way the detail of the text can tell us so much we would otherwise miss. Careful study opens up the wonders of God's Word!

Map of Third Missionary Journey

Test Yourself

1. What was special about a Roman colony?
2. Why did Paul go to Philippi?
3. What were the titles of two Roman officials in Philippi?
4. What indications were there that Lydia was a God-fearing person?
5. Why were Paul and Silas arrested?
6. Why did the jailor get ready to commit suicide?
7. How did the jailor know anything about the Gospel?
8. What is necessary before baptism?
9. In what way is baptism (a) a death; (b) a birth?
10. Why did Luke stay in Philippi?

For answers turn to page 42

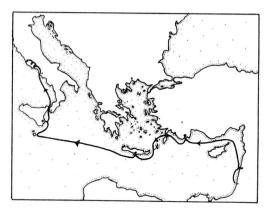

Map of Paul's Journey to Rome

Where was Paul writing from?

It seems most likely that Paul was writing from *Rome*, a number of years after the founding of the ecclesia at Philippi and his later visit recorded at the beginning of Acts 20.

We know for certain he was a *prisoner* (Philippians 1:7,13,14,17) but it was possible for people to come and see him. Acts describes a period of imprisonment in Rome,

"When he dwelt two whole years in his own hired house, and received all that came in unto him, preaching the kingdom of God, and teaching those things which concern the Lord Jesus Christ, with all confidence, no man forbidding him" (Acts 28:30,31).

It is likely that Paul's reputation for co-operation with the authorities and his Christ-like manner meant that at this stage he was not in a foul dungeon, though he would have to put up with being chained to a Roman soldier guarding him. It seems he took the opportunity to preach to his guards (Philippians 1:12,13).

Paul originally went to Rome as a prisoner following a near riot in Jerusalem when he preached the Gospel there (Acts 21:27 onwards). He tells us in his letter that he is about to face *trial* and may be released (Philippians 1:19-25), though the death sentence was a possibility for Christians in the 1st Century.

Contacts between Rome and Philippi

The distance by land and sea between Philippi and Rome was about 800 miles, roughly six weeks' journey in those days. We know that Timothy was with Paul in Rome. We can work out that the following journeys at least were made to maintain contact:

1. Messenger from Rome to Philippi to tell Philippians of Paul's imprisonment and need (Philippians 4:14).
2. Epaphroditus sent back with gifts (4:18).
3. Messenger takes news to Philippians of Epaphroditus' illness (2:26).
4. Return messenger reports effect of news on Philippians (2:26).
5. Epaphroditus' return home (2:25,28).
6. Paul hopes to send Timothy to them (2:19).
7. Timothy will have to return to Rome with news (2:19).
8. Paul himself hopes to be able to see them again (2:24).

Today we are used to being able to fly from one side of the world to the other in under 24 hours. In seconds we can dial anywhere in the world and speak to people. Yet are we any closer in our practical concern for each other than were these believers?

Earlier Contacts between Paul and the Philippians

These exchanges of news and practical assistance were typical of what had characterised the relationship between Paul and the Philippians from the outset, no doubt reflecting too the wonderful influence of Luke upon the young ecclesia.

Soon after leaving Philippi after the founding of the ecclesia described in Acts 16, the newly baptized believers sent a gift, probably of money, to assist in Paul's preaching in Thessalonica. They followed this up with a further gift. They realised the work had to go on! (Philippians 4:15,16).

It seems that when he reached Corinth, further assistance was given by the brethren and sisters in Macedonia (2 Corinthians 11:9), so that Paul could pay his way and get on with the work of preaching: "That which was lacking to me the brethren which came from Macedonia supplied: and in all things I have kept myself from being burdensome to you".

The spirit of this giving is summed up admirably in an earlier passage in the same letter (2 Corinthians 8:1-5). It was not that they were giving merely what was excess to their own requirements, Paul insists.

"Their abundance of joy and their extreme poverty have overflowed in a wealth of liberality on their part" (8:2, R.S.V.).

Real Generosity

The real test of generosity is when we give in a way which means we have to make sacrifices. In other words, we have to go without things we would like to have, to give up something we would rather have kept. This is also a test of our faith in God, for we demonstrate our willingness to trust that He will provide all we need. "First they gave themselves to the Lord," writes Paul (8:5). This is surely the response of those who accept that Christ has given all for them. If we give ourselves freely to the Lord's service, all that we are and have will be put at his disposal.

No wonder, as we shall see, there was such love and joy in the relationship between Paul and the Philippians. Their *fellowship* was not merely a matter of belonging to the same group. It was a real sharing of understanding and experience.

Test Yourself:

1. How did Paul witness when he was in prison?
2. What does he expect the result of his trial to be?
3. For what purpose was communication continued between the Philippians and Paul?
4. In what ways do you give for the work of the Lord?
5. Can you make a list of additional ways you could give? Which one are you going to start with?

For answers turn to page 43

FINDING YOUR WAY

The chapters in the Bible divide the letter up into four parts; but we can break it down into smaller sections and get a feeling for the overall development of Paul's thoughts. It will help to read the letter through at least twice in a modern version (say R.S.V. or N.I.V.), before returning to the A.V.

1: 1-2   *Opening Greetings*
My dear Philippians . . .

1: 3-11   *Paul's Prayer for the Ecclesia*
I'm so grateful to God for your practical help. May God richly bless you.

1:12-26   *Personal news about his imprisonment*
You'll be delighted to know that in spite of my imprisonment the Gospel is being preached. I can face anything, even death, knowing that I shall soon see Christ. But if I am released, I shall have the joy of coming to see you all again.

1:27-30   *Stand up for the Truth*
In the meantime stand together by the truth of the Gospel, come what may.

2:1-2:11   *Christ is the Supreme Example*
Try to agree with each other, even though some of you may have to give way. Remember how Christ showed perfect humility and is now Lord of all.

2:12-18   *Work out your Salvation*
Our aim is to be shining examples of true believers, ready for the day of Christ's appearing.

2:19-30   *News about Timothy and Epaphroditus and their plans*
I hope dear Timothy will be coming to you soon. Epaphroditus has been really helpful to me, but he has been so ill and missing you so much I have decided to send him home again. Give him a big welcome.

3:1-15   *Don't give way to the Judaizers*
Rejoice in the wonderful hope of the Gospel—don't be influenced by any false teachers trying to make you observe Jewish practices like circumcision. I was once a strict Jew, but I have gained everything by coming to Christ.

3:12-21   *Paul's living faith and hope*
Christ has made it possible for us to look forward to the glorious day of resurrection. Follow me in pressing forward to him; the false teachers are heading for destruction.

4:1-9   *Getting your priorities right*
Settle any differences among you and by prayer put all your concerns in the Lord's hands. The more you think about the qualities of the Lord's character, the less you'll worry about trivial things.

4:10-20   *Thanks for so much practical help*
In spite of all the problems I've had to face, I've learnt to be content by trusting God. But I really appreciated your gifts to me—as much as anything because they spoke of your love in Christ. May God richly reward you.

4:21-23   *Paul signs off*
All the brethren and sisters here send our love in the Lord to every one of you.
Your Brother by grace,
Paul.

CHAPTER ONE

OPENING GREETINGS 1:1-2

> *It was normal practice when Paul was writing to start off a letter with an elaborate greeting, saying who was writing and to whom. But normal practice takes on a new dimension when brethren in Christ write to each other!*

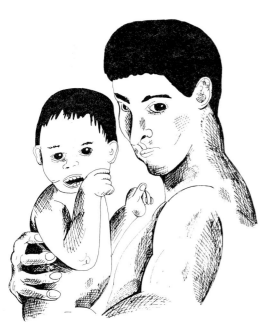

1: *Paul and Timothy*: a cross reference to Acts 16:1-5 reveals how Timothy came to join Paul on his missionary journey. He was clearly a young man in whom Paul saw great potential. We learn elsewhere that Timothy had been given an excellent grounding in the Old Testament by his grandmother and mother (2 Timothy 1:5; 3:15). They were Jews, but his father was a Greek (i.e. a Gentile). Timothy was circumcised so that he would not be rejected out of hand by the many Jews he and Paul were likely to meet. They wanted to be able to preach the Gospel to Jews as well as Gentiles, even though that very Gospel meant circumcision was no longer necessary.

Timothy had been with Paul when the Philippian ecclesia was founded (Acts 16:6-40), and Paul planned to send him to them again (2:19). To Paul, Timothy was like a son (2:22).

There are important lessons for us in this relationship. In the family of Christ all ages must learn from each other and help each other. The young can benefit so much from the experience and knowledge of age. The older ones should seek to involve the young, teaching not just by telling but by involving them in the work of the Lord. We learn more quickly by being shown than simply by being told. We learn by having a go ourselves, even if we make mistakes.

Saints: This certainly does not mean special people singled out for honour by the church because of their outstanding lives, and able to receive our prayers in heaven—an example of thoroughly unscriptural teaching. In the Bible saints are those who have been separated or made holy, or "sanctified" by Christ—in other words, all true believers who have been baptized. So Paul is writing to *all* the brethren and sisters in the ecclesia at Philippi.

Bishops and Deacons: bishop means "overseer", i.e. the elders of the meeting or arranging brethren, who have responsibility for managing the affairs of each ecclesia (see Acts 20:17,28; 1 Peter 5:1-4; 1 Timothy 3:1-11). In those days, before the New Testament was written and available for ecclesial guidance, the elders had gifts of the Holy Spirit to help them in their work. Deacons are those who serve the ecclesias in various practical ways, like looking after those in need (compare Acts 6:3). There are all kinds of jobs in the ecclesias for people who want to help. Are we willing to serve? (See 1 Timothy 3:13).

2: *Grace and peace:* grace is said to be a Gentile greeting and peace a Jewish one. Grace is God's mercy and loving gift to us when, as sinners, we deserve only death (Romans 6:23). Peace means wholeness—the bringing together of God and man through the grace of Jesus Christ (Ephesians 2:14-18). Grace and peace thus sum up the means and the end of salvation.

God our Father, and the Lord Jesus Christ: notice the two are distinct, though of course one in purpose. When Paul later wrote to Timothy, he emphasised "there is one God, and one mediator between God and men, the man Christ Jesus" (1 Timothy 2:5).

Test Yourself:

1. Why was Timothy a good choice for the work of preaching?
2. What is a saint?
3. Who are the equivalent of bishops in today's ecclesias?
4. What jobs being done by brethren and sisters in the ecclesia could you help with?
5. a) "By . . . are ye saved through faith; and that not of yourselves: it is the gift of God".
   b) "For he is our . . . , who hath made both one."

What are the missing words?

For answers turn to page 43

> *Paul thanks God for the fellowship with the Philippians which began at their conversion and has continued ever since. They have been constantly interested in his missionary work and have given financial support to him. They have been real sharers in his experiences. He prays that they will continue their spiritual growth "unto the glory and praise of God".*

3: The R.S.V. translation is: "I thank my God *in all* my remembrance of you"—in other words, all the time I think of you I am thankful to God.

4,5: *My prayers for you are always joyful, because of "your partnership in the gospel from the first day until now".*
Although Paul and Silas had a rough time in Philippi from the authorities, there was great satisfaction in the baptisms of Lydia and the jailor, along with their families (Acts 16:11-40). We are reminded there is joy in heaven "over one sinner that repenteth" (Luke 15:7,10). The new converts rejoiced too and opened up their homes to the apostle and his companions (Acts 16:34,40).

Understanding Fellowship

Fellowship begins with having something in common with someone. Once Lydia and the jailor's families had learnt and understood the essentials of the Gospel which Paul taught them, they were ready to commit themselves in faith to the new life in Christ. If, for example, they had been unable to believe that the Bible taught that "the wages of sin is death", and that Jesus died so that believers should not "perish", fellowship would not have been possible. If they had thought that you could believe in the hope of the resurrection, but reject the Bible's teaching about marriage, we cannot imagine that Paul would have allowed them to be baptized on the basis of a common faith.

The first requirement of fellowship therefore is to be "of one mind" (2:2) on the essential teachings or doctrines of the Word of God.

But this common mind is not just something to hold in your head. You enter into a "partnership" with God, the Lord Jesus and the members of the ecclesia. Just as a good family supports its members with practical acts of love and loyalty, so the ecclesial family requires regular contact, loving support and loyal commitment.

The Greek word Paul uses for fellowship (*koinōnia*) means all this, and the Philippian believers were wonderful examples of practical fellowship. They had

1. a common basis of belief
2. a common life together, showing forth the qualities of Christ's character, and
3. an appreciation that this meant giving of themselves and their possessions in the service of others.

The gifts they had sent to Paul to help his missionary work (4:14-18), see page 39, were real tokens of true fellowship.

6: Paul sees that God and the Lord Jesus are at work in believers through this fellowship. They are, of course, the power-house. If we can keep the fellowship alive, then "he which hath begun a good work in you will perform it until the day of Jesus Christ", i.e. the day of Christ's second coming, when loyal members of his family will be made "like him"—for ever! (3:20,21; 1 John 3:2).

7: *It is meet* (or right) *for me to think like this about you, because you are so dear to me. For both in my bonds* (the chains of his imprisonment) **and in the defence and confirmation of the Gospel** (standing up for the Truth against attackers and showing just how true it is) *you are all sharers with me of grace.*

The word "partakers" has the word for fellowship at its root. They haven't abandoned Paul because he is in prison and facing trial. A friend in need is a friend indeed.

When we are most aware of our need, we are open to receive God's grace. Paul learnt, through much hardship, the meaning of the phrase: "My grace is sufficient for thee: for my strength is made perfect in weakness" (2 Corinthians 12:9). We are all much more ready to turn to God in desperation than when we feel very satisfied with life. When we're up against a problem we can't solve, we're more likely to get on our knees. If we are honest with ourselves, every day and every hour we shall realise we need God's help. In the gift of Christ we see just how far God's grace can go.

Paul says that we receive God's grace, the blessing of His strength in fellowship, as we prayerfully seek Him on behalf of ourselves, and when we fellowship the sufferings of *others*. As the Philippians had entered into Paul's experience, they had shared the grace he was receiving to make him strong in his trials.

8: *God is my record* (witness) *that I really do long for you all with the deepest Christian love and feeling* ('*bowels*' indicates the seat of the affections). Notice the strength and quality of this feeling is because of their fellowship in Christ. The emotion comes *from* the fellowship—it doesn't create it.

9: Paul's prayers have involved thankful remembrance of the Philippians. He also asks God for further blessings for them—that their love may develop further, "in knowledge and all judgment (discernment, insight)". We have seen that our love of God and the Lord Jesus Christ must involve obedience to His Word and its demands. We need right thinking and judgement to guide us.

10: Then we shall be able to "approve things that are excellent" or "learn by experience the things that are most worthwhile" (see 4:8). This in turn leads to being "sincere and without offence", i.e. "pure and blameless" (R.S.V.). "Till the day of Christ", as in 1:6; 2:16; the day when Christ returns.

11: "The fruits of righteousness" have their origin in Christ—the perfect example of spiritual fruit which comes about by faith (Genesis 15:6) and in a pure and righteous life, one in harmony with God. See Galatians 5:22.

Understanding Prayer

We can learn much about *prayer* in this section. Prayer should begin with praise and thanksgiving for all the blessings we have from God. When we come to make requests, we should be trying to see how they fit in with what God wants for us — His will (contrast James 4:3). So the best we can ask for ourselves or for anyone else is that we can develop those right attitudes which enable us to turn every situation to spiritual advantage — and be better prepared for "the day of Christ".

Paul's prayer in verses 9-11 can be seen in five stages:

1. *Love* — positive response to God and His Word
2. *Knowledge and discernment* — right thinking and judgement
3. *Proving this knowledge* — in the testing ground of daily experience
4. *Sincerity* — the development of pure, wholesome minds
5. *Fruit* — the product: balanced, healthy characters, directed by Christ and giving glory to God

Five in Scripture is often associated with grace. These five stages are an apt summary of *grace in action*.

Test Yourself

1. Why is Paul so *thankful* to God for the Philippians?
2. Think of three aspects of *Fellowship*.
3. When is "the day of Christ"?
4. How were the Philippians "partakers of my grace"?
5. What should we start with in prayer?
6. Write out a list of things you can be *thankful* for and a list of *requests* to God on behalf of people you know. Do the requests link in with the principles of Paul's 5-fold prayer?
7. *Use* what you have thought about in (6) when you say your prayers *tonight*, before you get into bed.

For answers turn to page 43

PERSONAL NEWS ABOUT HIS IMPRISONMENT 1:12-26

> *Paul assures his readers that even though he is in prison, the situation has been turned to advantage for the Lord: the Gospel is being preached.*

Admittedly, some brethren are preaching from wrong motives, glad to put themselves forward while Paul is restric-·ted. But never mind—the preaching's the thing! Paul is not concerned about personal importance but about Christ being advanced. With trial before the Roman emperor ahead, he reflects on the advantages of life or death. He has no fear of death: the next moment will be the resurrection and Christ! Life will bring the possibility of being able to see his beloved Philippians again.

12,13: *Please understand that my imprisonment has meant the 'furtherance' or progress of the Gospel. For even though I'm chained to a guard, I've been able to witness for Christ to all sorts of people.* The ''palace'' is a reference to the praetorian guard, the personal bodyguard of the Roman emperor. It was a very large company and some of its members were assigned to guard Paul.

In Acts 28:30,31 we have a description of Paul in Rome, confined to a house, but free vigorously to preach the Gospel. We are reminded that it doesn't matter how difficult our circumstances, we can always witness to the Truth. Mud-hut, penthouse or bed-sitter will do; railway carriage, school field or shops. Wherever we are and whatever we are doing we are in fact

''manifesting'' or showing something. Is it always Christ?

14-17: Enthusiastic preaching is an encouragement to others. If we are good at it, we ought to try to take others with us to give them the idea. If we feel nervous, we can find someone to be with. Campaigns, Bible Reading groups and other opportunities can help us to build up our confidence.

Paul has made such an impact in Rome that it has spurred many more brethren to take advantage of his lead, some wanting to encourage him, especially since he is ''set for the defence of the gospel'', i.e. imprisoned as a result of his witness to the Lord. Others, regrettably, preach ''of contention, not sincerely, supposing to add affliction to my bonds'', i.e. ''out of personal rivalry, their motives not being pure, almost wanting my chain to give me even more pain and difficulty.''

It may be that some of these awkward brethren were simply jealous of Paul's great ability and influence. We are all prone to see people of talent and prominence as threats to our own self-esteem. Who are you jealous of? Who do you delight in criticising?

Or it may be that there were details of Paul's preaching and Scriptural understanding that some disagreed with. Amongst people dedicated to a distinctive set of beliefs based on the Word of God, there are bound to be disagreements, even though all meet on the basis of a common Statement of Faith. Matters like the interpretation of prophecy, versions of the Bible, even ways of praying or the choice of hymns can all command strongly felt, rival opinions. We need to understand that in any body of enthusiasts (especially religious enthusiasts!) such tensions are inevitable. But, like Paul, we must try to rise above them. A mature faith is able to discern what is central to the Gospel and what is not. And if we hold certain views strongly, let us not use them to undermine the preaching work of others. If there is a Christadelphian Campaign or Special Effort in a town it is a good thing. To have a rival one going on at the same time definitely is not.

18: Paul is content to feel that a spate of preaching is going on.

19: *"This preaching will contribute to my salvation"*, writes Paul. Some think "salvation" here means deliverance from imprisonment. It is hard to see how preaching will achieve that. He goes on to mention the further support of the prayers of the Philippians (which he presumably learnt about from Epaphroditus). Whom do we support in prayer on a regular basis?

All things work together for good

In addition he says he is helped by "the supply of the spirit of Jesus Christ". It has always been a source of strength to those suffering for the sake of the Gospel to know that their Lord did no less. The meek disposition of Jesus, who "for the joy that was set before him endured the cross, despising the shame", was an inspiration to Paul. He knew, too, that Jesus had said he was "a chosen vessel unto me, to bear my name before the gentiles, and kings, and the children of Israel: for I will show him how great things he must suffer for my name's sake" (Acts 9:15,16). For men of faith "all things work together for good". Whatever their circumstances, they "reckon that the sufferings of this present time are not worthy to be compared with the glory which shall be revealed in us" (Romans 8:28,18).

Paul is saying that the combination of preaching in Rome, prayers in Philippi and the "fellowship of the Lord's sufferings" (3:10)—the sense of sharing the experiences of Christ and being strengthened by showing the same disposition as his Lord—all this "shall turn to my salvation".

20: For his hope is that whatever the future holds—be it the death sentence or release—he will boldly witness for Christ, Christ will be "magnified" or honoured by his words and actions. Is this the hope and expectation of every one of us?

21: *"To me to live is Christ"*—the very centre of his being, the driving force of all his activity is Christ. And should death come, what is that but a short sleep and then the joy of being with Christ?

Nothing could be further from Paul's thoughts, of course, than the pagan idea of heaven-going. He knew full well that death meant the cutting off of life: "For in death there is no remembrance of thee: in the grave who shall give thee thanks" (Psalm 6:5). But for those baptized into Christ, who then "walk in newness of life", there is the belief that having "died with Christ", in baptism, "we shall also live with him, knowing that Christ being raised from the dead dieth no more"

(Romans 6:2-9). That hope of resurrection is to be fulfilled at the coming of Christ (see Philippians 3:11,20,21; 1 Corinthians 15:20-58; 2 Timothy 4:8; 1 John 3:2).

We see then how death can be ''gain'' to Paul. And what gain! To see an end of all his sufferings, his hardships, his trials, to see a world in which pain is removed, handicaps eliminated, the earth's resources all managed for the benefit of its inhabitants and ultimately no more death. What a hope this is, made sure by the promises of God and the resurrection of Christ! (Genesis 22:15-18; 2 Samuel 7:12-17; Isaiah 35; Daniel 12:2,3; 1 Corinthians 15:20-28; Revelation 20:4; 21:3,4).

22,23: No wonder Paul was *''in a strait betwixt two''* —hard-pressed as to whether life or death was best. Life would mean more work: *''fruitful labour for me''* (R.S.V.). Death would be like sleep. The next waking moment being the resurrection morning.

24-26: But characteristically Paul thinks not of himself first. However attractive the release of death, release to life will, he is convinced (*''having this confidence''*), open up the possibility of journeying to see the Philippians again, to further their joy and their faith. What a joyful reunion that would be!

Test yourself

1. Explain why Paul's ''bonds are manifest in all the palace''.

2. Can you think of any situation when you could not witness for Christ?

3. How is it possible to preach Christ ''in pretence''?

4. From 1 Corinthians 15:20-28 and other passages listed above, make a short timetable of events at the return of Christ.

5. Make a list of reasons why you would like to ''be with Christ''. What reasons have you for wanting to ''remain in the flesh''?

For answers turn to page 43

> *Paul urges the Philippians to be true citizens of the Kingdom of God. Whatever the cost to them in persecution from enemies of the Gospel, they must stand together for the Truth.*

27: *Only* ("whatever happens" — J.B.P.) *let your conversation* (way of life) *be as it becometh* ("worthy of", R.V.) *the Gospel of Christ.*

The Greek word Paul uses, which the A.V. translates "conversation", literally means *citizenship*. Remember that Philippi was a Roman colony and very proud of its civic arrangements (Acts 16:12,21). Paul's choice of words reminds the brethren and sisters that they are not concerned with the politics of earth but the citizenship of heaven (see 3:20). God's servants are "strangers and pilgrims" for the time being, looking forward to "a city which hath foundations, whose builder and maker is God" (Hebrews 11:10, 13-16).

Christadelphians, because they do not vote for any political party or fight for any régime anywhere, are a truly international community. There is no risk of one brother fighting against another brother on opposite sides of a political divide and brethren and sisters cannot be refused entry to a country on political grounds. This does not mean that in all other respects they ignore the laws of each country. Rather they are at pains to be subject to the authorities and obey their laws — so long as these are not in conflict with the higher laws of God (Romans 13:1-7; John 18:36; Acts 5:29).

Here Paul is emphasising that as citizens of *God's* kingdom, the way we live must be a true reflection of the teaching of the One whom God has anointed as its king.

"Stand fast in one spirit, with one mind striving together for the faith of the gospel". The picture is of an army which stands its ground when under attack. In battle its soldiers fight together, with a common aim, as comrades supporting each other.

28: *Don't be frightened by your opponents. Your steadfastness will be proof of their certain destruction* (A.V. "evident token of perdition") *but also proof of your salvation.*

29,30: *Your faith in and suffering for Christ is like a gracious gift* (A.V. "it is given"). *The conflict you are experiencing is just the sort of thing which you saw when I preached to you in Philippi and which you know I am having to endure here in Rome.*

How vividly the Philippians would have remembered the beating Paul and Silas received in their city and the way they were flung into the prison and fastened in the stocks. The jailor later washed their wounds, immediately before he washed away his own sins in baptism (Acts 16:22,23). No doubt the new brethren received insults following their baptisms into Christ. Perhaps the jailor had to leave his job, if the authorities took seriously the view expressed in Thessalonica: "These all do contrary to the decrees of Caesar (the Roman emperor), saying there is another king, one Jesus'' (Acts 17:7). It was not of course true that they were not law-abiding. In fact their standards in this respect were now likely to be higher. But Christianity was viewed as a subversive religion, with revolutionary implications.

Bold for Christ

Today it is not at all easy in some countries to stand for the Truth. Many brethren and sisters have to live out their beliefs in the face of considerable pressures of one kind or another. Even in those countries where there has been a strong Christian tradition of some kind, what is taught as Christianity bears little relationship to the Bible and is often more concerned with social aims. In schools a multi-cultural approach has resulted in the Christian faith being looked upon as an interesting option amongst a whole range of world religions and life-styles. The Christian view of family life is no longer the norm. For most people economic and material prosperity *now* are far more important than citizenship of the Kingdom of God.

In seeking to understand the true nature of the Gospel taught by Christ and the apostles, we shall have to live with scorn and derision—for we are very unfashionable. We are considered narrow-minded for not going along with the majority. Persecution could be round the corner.

Paul's message to the Philippians to stand by the faith they had learnt from the Word of God and to trust that God's grace was sufficient to sustain them, come what may—this message is for *us* too.

Test Yourself

1. What does Paul mean by ''conversation'' in 1:27?
2. What, in brief, does he mean by ''the faith of the gospel''?
3. Why does he say it is *given* to us to suffer for Christ?

For answers turn to page 44

CHAPTER TWO

CHRIST IS THE SUPREME EXAMPLE 2:1-11

> *They must avoid unprofitable arguments and give way to each other for the sake of unity. Christ's example of perfect humility is the ideal model. His humility led to the cross. But God has raised him to be Lord of all.*

1: Paul has been urging his readers to stand together in defence of their faith. This keeping together requires Christ-like qualities. We are all different and the differences between us can cause friction. It requires real effort and a readiness to sink what *we* want, if we are to succeed in our relationships with others. It requires too a readiness to put God and His word before our own opinions and ideas.

So in verse 1 he is saying, **"If you have appreciated the tender, reassuring and kindly characteristics of the Lord Jesus, if you have grasped that your fellowship together is based on all you have learnt from the Word of God, which in itself has developed spiritual qualities in you** . . .

2: . . . *complete my joy by maintaining unity in the ecclesia."* It is important to grasp that unity comes from a common understanding of the Word of God.

"Fellowship of the spirit" is seen by some today as an experience which brings people together whatever their differences of outlook, and regardless of whether their thinking is in harmony with the will of God. It is clear from Philippians that fellowship began when the families in Philippi were baptized, after they had listened to the Word of God being explained to them and had agreed that the apostle Paul's teaching was what they believed (see notes on 1:5). Paul believed the Bible was the inspired Word of God and contained all that was needed for salvation (2 Timothy 3:15,16). "Fellowship of the spirit" cannot be separated from fellowship which starts from accepting without reservation what the Spirit-inspired writings of the Bible have to tell us about God and His purpose.

The *joy* Paul refers to here, and so often in this letter, is also something which arises *out* of this unity of mind.

The basis of unity must be submission to what God tells us in His word (Isaiah 66:2). We sometimes refer to the essential doctrines as "first principles". Paul was well aware that in time there would be false teachers who would try to distort the teaching of Jesus and the apostles (Acts 20:29,30; 2 Timothy 4:3,4). Here and elsewhere he urges his readers to stand by the *Truth* which has been committed to them (1:27; 3:17; 1 Timothy 6:20; 2 Timothy 1:13).

3: **"Strife and vainglory"** implies trying to form rival groups which take away from the unity of the ecclesia. The basis of this is usually pride—when people are convinced that they alone know best. Or it can be jealousy—we simply want to work off a grudge against someone, like some of those preaching in competition with

Paul (1:15). It is sad to realise that this can happen even amongst the best of brethren and sisters.

"In lowliness of mind let each esteem other better than himself." Be humble enough to believe that you are not always right. You can learn a good deal from your brethren and sisters.

4: "Don't feel the world has got to revolve around you. Put other people before yourself."

5: "Try to have the same mentality as Christ . . .

6: who, in spite of having status or rank as the Son of God, did not try to make out he was equal with God, but rather

7: emptied himself of any pride and took it upon himself to be the servant of others, making himself experience what being human was like."

The paraphrase above attempts to bring out the sense of these verses as simply as possible.

"Being in the form of God" balances out "the form of a servant". Because Jesus was the Son of God, he naturally showed forth to men what God was like. He was "full of grace and truth" (John 1:14); everything about the Lord Jesus Christ helps us to understand what God is like. We sometimes say a son is "the spit-image" of his father. So Jesus could say, "He that hath seen me hath seen the Father". But he also emphasised: "My Father is greater than I". He made clear his dependence on his Father in all things. He never "grasped at equality with God", as though equality was some prize to be carried off. That was what the serpent suggested Adam and Eve might do: "Ye shall be as gods," it said (Genesis 3:5). Human efforts to be like God are the root of human trouble. Pride comes before a fall. Jesus knew that as a Son he must be obedient (Hebrews 5:8).

Bringing together God and Man

The wonderful thing about the person of Jesus was that he perfectly shows us what God is like, yet he was actually born of a human mother and shared our nature. "The children of a family share the same flesh and blood; and so he too shared ours" (Hebrews 2:14 N.E.B.). It is precisely because Jesus was born with the same feelings and impulses as us, and therefore "was in all points tempted like as we are, *yet without sin*" (Hebrews 4:15), that he is able to be our representative. He was one of us, yet he overcame our tendency to sin and submitted to his Father's will completely.

If God had ignored human sin, we would have been left in a helpless state, doomed to continue for ever making a mess of the world and a misery of so many lives. God wants us to realise how harmful sin is. In the perfect life of Jesus we see the contrast between the life of God and the sinful life of man.

But God wants to forgive us. He does so by telling us that if we join ourselves to His Son (which we do when we are baptized), then we shall be demonstrating that we understand our need to turn away from sin. Because Christ did not sin, he was able to be raised from the death he experienced because he shared our nature. He is now able to live eternally with God. Through Christ then, we can share the same hope—of being like him, and thus like God (John 17:19-21; Romans 5:1; Hebrews 2:17; 1 John 1:5-10).

What we have been attempting to describe is referred to as the *Atonement*. The word almost explains itself—it is about making God and mankind *at one*. The diagram may help:

GOD — *perfect, too pure to behold*
| *evil*

JESUS*, Son of God and Son of Man*
| *— made like man, but lived*
| *for God*

MAN—*imperfect and sinful*

It is Jesus Christ, both Son of God and Son of Man, who is able to bring together God and man.

No-one can adequately express the wonder of this method of providing for man's salvation. No-one can adequately express the wonderful and glorious achievement of Jesus. But Paul continues in verses 8-11 by stating that the love and obedience of Jesus, which reached its climax when he laid down his life on the cross, enabled his Father to raise him to a new and glorious life, to make him the foundation stone of the ecclesias, the mediator for all mankind and the king of all creation. Eventually, when Christ has established the kingdom of God on earth and is reigning from Jerusalem, all men will acknowledge him as king. And by this means, they will give glory to God (Psalm 72; Isaiah 2:2-4; Zechariah 14:9,16; Luke 1:32,33; 1 Corinthians 15:25-28; Revelation 7:9-11).

Is Jesus Christ *our* Lord *now*, to the glory of God the Father?

Test Yourself

1. What is necessary for believers to be "of one mind" in Christ?

2. Explain "thought it not robbery to be equal with God."

3. Why was it necessary for Jesus to be born as a man?

4. How was Jesus a *servant*?

5. If you confess that "Jesus is Lord", what practical effect should that have?

6. Who do you find it difficult to get on with? Try to make a list of the things that cause the problem. What can *you* do to help?

7. On the basis of some of the Bible passages listed above, how would you describe what it will be like in the kingdom of God?

For answers turn to page 44,45

Paul exhorts (or encourages) the Philippians to show the same spirit of obedience to God as the Lord Jesus. Then God can work through them. Arguments will only distract from the effectiveness of their witness to the Truth. When Christ returns, Paul hopes to rejoice that his efforts in preaching to the Philippians have not been wasted. Even if he is sentenced to death for his preaching, there is still cause for rejoicing in the opportunity to witness for Christ.

12: *"Wherefore"*—in the light of what Paul has been writing about the complete obedience of Christ, his followers must also submit to God in all things, whether Paul is visiting them or not. Most of us find it easier to be on our best behaviour on special occasions. It's not so easy when you're on your own to keep up the standard of Christ!

"Work out your own salvation with fear and trembling". Throughout his life Jesus had to wrestle against the inclination to please himself and to conform to people's expectations of what he should do. The strain was at its most intense as the cross drew near. "Father, if thou be willing, remove this cup from me", he prayed in Gethsemane, "nevertheless not my will, but thine be done" (Luke 22:42). God strengthened Jesus with the help of the angels and he was able to go through the suffering which led to his death (see Hebrews 5:7-9). "Fear and trembling" indicates the spirit of total reverence and submission to Almighty God. There is no place for the casual here. That is why the way we dress, the way we behave and the way we speak are all important. When we go to the meeting we are assembling with the ecclesia to worship the King of creation. We should feel sufficiently in awe to want to put on our best clothes and to be on our best behaviour. When we talk to God in prayer, we are in a position of mighty privilege—which we do not deserve. It is not appropriate to be "chatty" or to use the kind of slang so popular around us.

Faith and Work

So in every aspect of our lives we must "work out our salvation". Of course we are saved by *faith*. We cannot earn forgiveness of sins by doing this, that or the other. But our faith is not genuine if we do not try to please God in lives of obedience. It is not enough to say, "I believe in baptism"; we must be baptized. It is not enough to say, "I believe that Christ will come again"; we must get ready. It is not enough to say, "I believe in the judgement seat of Christ"; for "every man's work shall be made manifest: for the day shall declare it . . . and the fire shall try every man's work of what sort it is" (1 Corinthians 3:13).

James tells us that "faith without works is dead" (James 2:26). The whole relationship between *faith* and *works* is admirably summed up in Ephesians 2:8-10 (R.S.V.).

"For by grace you have been saved through faith; and this is not your own doing, it is the gift of God—not

because of works, lest any man should boast. For we are his workmanship, created in Christ Jesus for good works, which God prepared beforehand, that we should walk in them.''

13: "For it is God which worketh in you". Again there is the emphasis on God's will being done. It is not doing what we think is good, or what others say is good. It is what God requires. Only from His word can we find that out. The Greek word "to work" is literally "to energise". Our faith in God and relationship with Him through Jesus provides the power for action.

14: But it is action *together*. No arguments or fuss! Over and over again Paul emphasises the need to work as a team. If you've ever seen a good 'eight' of oarsmen rowing, you have seen an excellent example of teamwork. The boat moves forward with power because the eight are in complete harmony. It only wants one person to be out of rhythm and the balance and efficiency of the whole boat are affected.

15: "that you may be blameless and harmless—beyond criticism, innocent of nasty intentions, sincere". Argument, criticism, insisting on your own way—this will undermine the effectiveness of the ecclesia. Don't rock the boat!

For we are **"in the midst of a crooked and perverse nation (R.V. 'generation')"** i.e. the standards of the world around us are not helpful to maintaining the standards of Christ. We need to help each other, not get at each other, for we must **"shine as lights".** Do people notice the difference? We may not be aware of the

effect. But in a totally dark place, even the tiniest flame from a match can be seen everywhere.

16: "holding forth the word of life" (or "holding fast"). Notice again the stress placed on the connection between effective witness and the word of God. "Thy word is a lamp unto my feet, and a light unto my path", writes the Psalmist (Psalm 119:105). We must be true and loyal to the word of God, as was Christ—"the word made flesh", "the light of the world".

"that I may rejoice . . . " Paul hopes that as a result of the continued faithfulness of the Philippians, we will be able to rejoice when Christ returns, for he will see the fruits of his work with them— they will be rewarded with eternal life (see Matthew 25:23).

17: "If we be offered upon the sacrifice and service of your faith". Paul is thinking of the possibility of having to die for his faith in Rome. He reflects that this will be like pouring out his blood over the sacrifice which the Philippians are making in offering themselves completely to the service of God. Under the law of Moses, animals, food and drink were offered to God as tokens of repentance from sin and dedication to God. These rituals were like shadows of the true offering of a perfect life—seen in the Lord Jesus Christ (see Hebrews 10:1-10). The joy in such a sacrifice, which Paul invites the Philippians to share with him (verse 18), is because it is a means to an end. In the Book of Revelation we read: "Blessed are the dead which die in the Lord . . . that they may rest from their labours; and their works do follow them" (Revelation 14:13).

Test Yourself

1. Explain the relationship between *faith* and *works*.

2. How does God work in us?

3. Can you think of any complaints or criticisms you have made lately about the ecclesia? Did they help to build up the ecclesia? If not, how can you stop being a moaner and complainer?

4. What will cause Paul to "rejoice in the day of Christ?

5. How can Paul be offered upon the sacrifice of the Philippians' faith?

For answers turn to page 45

NEWS ABOUT TIMOTHY AND EPAPHRODITUS
AND THEIR PLANS 2:19-30

> *Paul hopes to send Timothy from Rome to Philippi soon. Timothy is a fine example of Christian faith. Paul trusts he too may be able to come to see them. He intends to send Epaphroditus home to Philippi. Epaphroditus came to give Paul as much help as possible, but he has been seriously ill and worried about the folk back home. Paul will be happy for him to get home safely. After all he has gone through, Epaphroditus deserves the warmest welcome in Philippi.*

19: Paul is constantly concerned for the well-being of his converts. Although it will take months to get news back, he is still really keen to send Timothy to find out how things are in Philippi.

20: Nobody is *"like-minded"*, or so close to his own thinking, and it is second nature to him to be genuinely concerned about their welfare.

21: *So many are only interested in themselves, not the work of the Lord.* Here is a challenge indeed to us! Which category are we in? Concern for those in the ecclesia or only for ourselves? And what about the ecclesia worldwide? Do we enter into the problems and experiences of our brethren and sisters in far off places whom we cannot regularly see? Through the pages of *The Christadelphian* or *The Bible Missionary* we can get to know about them. Or are we more interested in reading *The News of the World* or seeing it on TV?

Everyone of us should support our own magazines, and through them, and other means, try to build up the ecclesia worldwide. There are people to write to, people to pray for, people who need practical assistance, such as that ministered by the Bible Mission Welfare Fund. Within our own countries there are many ecclesias which need help and many of the brotherhood's organisations which deserve our support. Do we care for their state?

22: *"Ye know the proof of him"* — R.S.V.: *"Timothy's worth ye know"*. More often in simpler societies like that of the First Century, a son followed in his father's footsteps, learning the same trade or continuing in the same job. He learnt from and alongside his father. So Timothy has learnt the work of a missionary from Paul.

22,23: Paul implies here that he will soon know if he is to be released from imprisonment or not.

25: *I feel I must send Epaphroditus back to you.* What a tribute he now pays to Epaphroditus; he describes him as:

1. brother, i.e. brother in the Lord
2. companion in labour, i.e. fellow-worker
3. fellow soldier, i.e. he has "fought a good fight" for the gospel alongside me (see Ephesians 6:10-17; 2 Timothy 4:7)

In addition Epaphroditus was

> 4. your messenger (Greek *apostle*) —sent to Paul by them
>
> 5. he that ministered to my wants (needs). He came to Paul bringing a gift from the ecclesia at Philippi (4:18) and with the intention of cheering Paul in his imprisonment.

26: Epaphroditus has missed the Philippians back home, especially as he has suffered a serious illness. Note that his concern was more for the effect that news of his illness might have on the Philippians! We are again reminded of the importance of consideration for others, especially those who are likely to be anxious about us.

27: God showed mercy to Epaphroditus for he was spared from death. Paul was spared the sorrow such a tragedy would have caused.

28: R.S.V.: *"I am the more eager to send him therefore"* (He has not yet left). Paul will be glad in the happiness of Epaphroditus and the Philippians.

29,30: *Welcome him in the Lord* (almost as though he were the Lord!) *and be appreciative of the sacrifice he has made in making such a journey in the service of others, and in the course of it nearly losing his life.* "In reputation"—in honour. Paul is anxious they should not feel Epaphroditus has failed in his mission to Paul.

"To supply your lack of service toward me"—this does not mean they were at fault, but that Epaphroditus did what distance prevented them all from doing: and he risked his life in the process.

Throughout this chapter there has been an emphasis on *service*. Christ is the supreme example, but Paul, Timothy and Epaphroditus have all likewise been seeking the wellbeing of the household of faith, God's family, above their own comfort.

This is a very high standard to follow. In our ecclesias today there are some who seem all the time to give to the service of the Truth. Others seem always to be missing when help is needed. How do *we* each serve our brethren and sisters in the ecclesia?

> **Test Yourself**
>
> 1. What did Paul mean in writing that Timothy was "like-minded"?
>
> 2. Why was Epaphroditus "full of heaviness"?
>
> 3. What did Paul mean about Epaphroditus supplying their "lack of service"?
>
> 4. Make a list of ways in which you have served the ecclesia in the last week. How could you improve on this standard?
>
> 5. How could you show concern for brethren and sisters in other lands?
>
> *For answers turn to page 45*

CHAPTER THREE

DON'T GIVE WAY TO THE JUDAIZERS 3:1-11

Our rejoicing is in the Lord. Therefore, although Paul has said it many times before, he must stress again that it is no use going back to the rituals of the law, like circumcision. Paul had been brought up as a strict Jew. But he left Judaism for the blessings of faith in Christ.

1: *"Finally"* seems to mean "furthermore" (as in 1 Thessalonians 4:1; 2 Thessalonians 3:1). Paul is moving on to his next point. "Rejoice in the Lord" emphasises what Paul is leading up to in the chapter. By contrast, he must first warn about the Judaizers.

Christ and the Law of Moses

Since the Christian faith has its origin in the Jewish faith (it is indeed "the hope of Israel"), it was inevitable that even converts to Christ who were Jews had difficulty in throwing off much of their Jewish origins. Not that "the law and the prophets", the Old Testament Scriptures, were any less relevant now. But as a result of the coming of Christ their full significance could be understood.

But because Christ fulfilled the law, since he was perfectly obedient to his Father, its ritual requirements were no longer necessary, e.g. sacrifices, ritual washings, sabbath day observance (keeping Saturday as a day of rest in which no form of work at all could be done). No longer were the temple and the priests needed. For Christ was now the true High Priest in heaven and no other priests were necessary. Baptized believers in Christ were now "the temple of the living God"—a spiritual temple in which God, through Christ, could truly live. The literal temple in Jerusalem was going to be destroyed—and it was in A.D. 70.

Christ had called Paul to be an apostle to the Gentiles. He was anxious that no barriers should be placed in the way of Gentile converts, and at an important conference in Jerusalem this had been agreed (Acts 15). But what people agree in the atmosphere of a conference or special meeting sometimes turns out to be very different from what they do when they get home, or what others will do whom they represented. So Paul constantly faced difficulties from Jews trying to stop the spread of Christianity and from Jews converted to Christianity, who still tried to make Gentile Christians conform to Jewish customs.

Of these customs, *circumcision* was the cause of greatest conflict. For an explanation of circumcision look up Genesis 17:9-14. The point is made in the New Testament that circumcision involved cutting away the flesh (the foreskin) of the male organ needed for reproduction. It was a vivid reminder that the children of God came into existence not by human means, but by the action of God. What's more, "flesh" is contrasted with "spirit" in the Bible; the one reminds of man's earthly, selfish desires, the other his godly spiritual potential. In Romans, Paul argues that a real Jew has cut away in symbol his fleshly desires, not just his actual, literal flesh (Romans 2:25-29). Literal circumcision is not demanded of those who strive to follow Christ.

We can now return to the text of Philippians 3!

1: *"To write . . . "* Paul doesn't mind keeping on repeating the points to follow. He has told the Philippians before, but he feels it is safer to remind them yet again.

2: *"Beware of the dogs"*—not a very complimentary term, but one which was usually reserved by the Jews for the Gentiles. Paul has turned it around, calling the Jews "dogs" who are insisting that Gentile Christians must be circumcised. ("Concision" = the cutters off! They were wanting to cut off the flesh—literally—and thereby cut off the Gentiles from the family of God).

3: By worshipping God according to the spiritual principles of His word as fully revealed by Christ, we demonstrate what circumcision should be all about. This is far more important than thinking salvation comes just by the circumcision of the flesh.

4-6: Paul now reminds them that actually nobody could have been a stricter Jew than he; he was a model Pharisee (the Pharisees were a leading Jewish sect who rigorously upheld the law of Moses, according to the strict traditions of their ancestors); he had conducted a vigorous campaign as a young man *against* the early Christian believers.

7: But all the advantages he had gained from a first-class training as a Pharisee and the prospect of an excellent career, he cast aside with absolutely no regrets after his conversion (described in Acts 9:1-30).

The Excellency of Knowing Christ

8: Paul stresses how strongly he feels about the excellence of knowing Christ contrasted with the waste of any other approach to life. Particularly when we are young, there are many things in the world around us which are attractive. But the more we appreciate the real quality of life in Christ, the more we learn that there is simply *nothing* which will compare to it. Everything else can be classed as "dung"—refuse, garbage.

9: For in Christ we can be forgiven our sinfulness, thus enabling us to enter into a relationship with God. (Remember the point about the atonement? We can't be "at one" with God—who is completely righteous, while we are sinners.) For the Jews, life was one long burden of trying to make sure you carried out every rule and regulation devised by people like the Pharisees in an attempt to fulfil the law of Moses perfectly. But it couldn't be done (see Acts 13:39). It was actually impossible for mere men to match God's righteousness.

What a relief to face up to this fact and to realise that Christ, by his perfect obedience to God, in fulfilment of what the law was really all about, had taken away the burden. Now, by faith in Christ demonstrated in repentance and baptism anybody, Jew or Gentile, could be counted righteous before God (Romans 3:20-24; Galatians 3:19-29).

Knowing Christ

10: As a result he could now enjoy the benefit of a relationship with Jesus of the closest kind. "Know him" means not simply "know about him" or "be acquainted with him". It carries the idea of a deep understanding. Because of this closeness, Paul can identify with "the power of his resurrection"—that is, the living influence of the risen Christ; "the fellowship of his sufferings", i.e. by suffering for Christ (see 1:29) and "being made conformable unto his death", i.e. linking ourselves to the sacrifice of Christ. If we "conform" to something, it means that we go along with it, e.g. we may conform to school regulations—we don't try to buck the system! In this case, we conform to the death of Christ by associating ourselves with it in baptism, and thereafter week by week in the breaking of bread, or memorial service (because we "remember" the Lord's death). (See Romans 6:4-6; John 6:53,54; Luke 22:17-20; 1 Corinthians 10:26).

11: It is clear from the references just listed, that by this association with Christ we make possible for ourselves the hope of the resurrection. The "dying" now is not just the outward act of baptism, or the regular weekly meeting together on the first day of the week, or at other times for the breaking of bread service. These things must be done, but if they become mere outward show, they would be like circumcision had become for the Jews—

a rite with no meaning. If we are truly "dead" with Christ, it means that we have declared we no longer wish to be sinners. The direction of our life will now be Christ-wards. He has made possible the forgiveness of our sins. We must strive to let God work in us (2:13) so that the character of Christ shines through us and we effectively witness to the gospel (2:16).

Test Yourself

1. What is "not grievous" to Paul (verse 1)?

2. What *should* circumcision stand for?

3. What is meant by "the righteousness of the law"?

4. How do believers associate themselves with the death and resurrection of Christ?

5. Look up Galatians 5:16-25 and make a list of the works of the flesh and the fruit of the spirit, using modern language as far as possible. How do these relate to the life of Jesus?

For answers turn to page 46

PAUL'S LIVING FAITH AND HOPE 3:12-21

> *Since Christ has made it possible for us to win the prize, let's press on, without wavering, to gain it. You have seen how I turned my back on the past. You must do the same, ignoring people whose aims are really selfish. We must live now like citizens of heaven. When Jesus returns to the earth, he will reward us by changing us to be like him—no more sin, no more pain or death!*

12: Paul wants to emphasise that although he has obtained forgiveness of sins through Christ, that does not mean he now no longer sins. He must keep trying his best to be worthy of all that Christ has made possible. "He that endureth to the end shall be saved" (Matthew 10:22). We must be careful to distinguish between our thankfulness and joy in salvation *now* and our recognition that salvation is a process which is not completed until after the judgement.

"Apprehended" means "seized". Christ "took hold" of Paul on the road to Damascus. After a period in which Paul was fighting against the Truth and trying not to face up to its enormous implications for him, he saw that the living Lord was real. Paul now hopes to "take hold" of that eternal salvation which Christ "took hold" of him to make possible.

13,14: Again Paul stresses that he has not yet obtained salvation in its fulness. But he is putting the past behind him and constantly "straining forward" (R.S.V.) to what lies ahead.

It is no use bemoaning the past, or dwelling on sins that have been committed. We must confess them and believe that in Christ they can be forgiven (see 1 John 1:9). Then, with eyes set on the kingdom, we must press forward doing our best. Great effort is involved. The words used are associated with athletics. The successful runner is dedicated in his training and commitment to winning the next race. So too we must "seek first the kingdom of God and his righteousness". Everything must come second to that aim.

The runner has his eyes set on the finishing tape. Like Christ who, "for the joy that was set before him endured the cross, despising the shame" (Hebrews 12:2), we too must fix our sights on Christ, knowing that the prize will be the "high" or "upward" calling of God, i.e. God will invite us to share His glorious nature; we shall be like Christ in his perfect, resurrected state (Matthew 25: 23,34; 1 Corinthians 15:53-58; 1 John 3:1-3).

15: *If we have a mature* (A.V. "perfect") *faith, we shall understand this need to keep on striving,* to press forward, putting the past behind us. Those who don't yet understand, God will enlighten.

16: R.S.V. *"Only let us hold true to what we have attained",* i.e. as we make progress in our spiritual lives, let us take courage and move forward together.

7: The Philippians have some fine examples of Christian faith in action in the apostle Paul and his companions; men like Silas, Timothy and Luke. Paul is not boasting. He is encouraging his readers. They can see he is not just a *talker*. He is a *doer*. "Ensample" = example (Greek "type").

18,19: Paul has often warned against those whose discipleship becomes a form of self-indulgence. It is with deep regret ("even weeping") that he has to brand them ***"enemies of the cross of Christ"***. The cross is about self-sacrifice. When we are baptized into Christ we identify ourselves with that sacrifice and "put on" the selfless life of Christ. If we later allow our selfish instincts (our "belly") to rule our actions, we "crucify . . . the Son of God afresh" (Hebrews 6:6). The "works of the flesh" are listed in Galatians 5:19-21. Besides obvious sins of self-indulgence, like fornication or drunkenness, strife is listed and "heresy" — which means creating splinter-groups by teaching different doctrines from those which are sound and well established. Many problems in ecclesial life are caused by people who are self-indulgent in their thinking and try to inflict their views on the rest. Read Colossians 3:1-17 to see the contrast between earthly, fleshly attitudes and the true qualities of a spiritually-minded person.

20,21: *"Conversation"* = citizenship or manner of life (see 1:27). Notice how Paul emphasises the true Christian faith and hope. *Now* we must try to live as citizens of heaven, i.e. our thinking, speaking and manner of life must be directed by Christ our King. Our hope for the *future* is not to go to heaven, but to be rewarded when Christ returns to the earth (1 Corinthians 15:23). For then our "vile body" — the source of fleshly, earthly thoughts and actions, will be transformed by the power of Christ (1 Corinthians 15:24-26) to be "like unto his glorious body".

The Wonders of Immortality

When we read the accounts of the resurrection appearances of Jesus, we realise that there was an altogether different dimension to Christ's spiritual body. He could still be visible, could eat, could show the marks on his hands from the crucifixion. But he could move through space and time in a way we can hardly comprehend (Luke 24:36-43). Now all pain and suffering was past. The strains of the 3½ years' ministry which led up to his death must have made him look prematurely aged and gaunt (Isaiah 53:2,3). But no doubt in resurrection his youth was renewed (Isaiah 40:31). In fact he was barely recognisable to those who had known him (John 20:14; Luke 24:16). But best of all, the tendency to want to satisfy the flesh, the selfish instincts inherited from his human mother, was now removed (Hebrews 2:14-18; 4:15).

The same wonderful prospect is promised to those who are looking for the appearing again from heaven of the Lord Jesus Christ. Then, our physical disabilities, the effects of age and natural decay, will no longer wear us down. Then our characters will quite readily show forth "love, joy, peace, longsuffering, gentleness, goodness, faith, meekness, self-control". For sin will have no place in those given immortal lives.

This was the prospect which fired the apostle Paul with such enthusiasm, and for which he was prepared to sacrifice everything. It should have the same effect on us!

Test Yourself

1. What does "apprehend" mean (verses 12,13)?

2. What lesson does Paul take from an athlete?

3. What is "the high calling of God"?

4. What does the following mean: "mark them which walk so as ye have us for an example"?

5. What changes will take place in those made immortal?

For answers turn to page 46

CHAPTER FOUR

GETTING YOUR PRIORITIES RIGHT 4:1-9

> *With the prize of eternal life before you, hold on to your faith.*
>
> *Please, sisters Euodias and Syntyche, agree with one another. Help them to do this.*
>
> *Rejoice in the Lord and bring everything to him in prayer—then you need have no anxieties about anything.*
>
> *Keep uppermost in your minds the wonderful qualities of God's character and try to remember the things I have shown you.*

1: Paul's deep feeling for the brethren and sisters in Philippi is emphasised in this verse. **"Crown"** refers to the leafy wreaths which were placed on the heads of those who were victorious in athletic events like the Olympic Games. Paul's preaching work is rewarded by the successful establishment of such a fine ecclesia: the Philippians are like a victor's crown—or gold medal—to him.

"Stand fast"—as in 1:27. Don't water down or set on one side the essential teachings of the Bible. Let your house be built upon the rock of hearing and doing the words of Christ!

2,3: Euodias and Syntyche were two sisters in the ecclesia who obviously were having a disagreement. We know nothing about what it was, but Paul appeals to them to agree **"in the Lord"**. Imagine how red-faced they must have been to hear themselves referred to like this when the

letter was read out in the ecclesia! In chapter 2:1-11 we saw the basis of unity in the ecclesia: a common understanding of the Word of God (such as is enshrined in the Christadelphian Statement of Faith) and Christ-like attitudes which enable each to submit in love to the other. Human beings very easily fall out with each other, and often the basis of disagreement is pride and jealousy. "In the Lord" there is no room for either of these traits.

We do not know who was the **"true yoke-fellow"** (someone who shares a burden or task) even though many names have been suggested. There is an emphasis in the verse on *fellowship*. If we are busy working with others in the ecclesia, we are much less likely to be falling out with one another. If we think of all in the ecclesia as people "for whom Christ died", then we shall wish to serve and help them, as Christ has done! If we are aware of disagreements we should try to assist in resolving them, rather than taking sides, or spreading gossip about the problem. Often the best course of action is to keep the matter to yourself and prayerfully try to encourage the right kind of positive atmosphere in which agreement can be reached.

It is comforting to know that even in an ecclesia as spiritually strong as Philippi, there were difficulties. We should try to be mature enough to recognise that such difficulties are not a reflection on the essential truths of the Gospel, but of human nature not yet transformed into the likeness of Christ.

4: **_"Rejoice in the Lord alway"_** is a recurring theme in the letter. But it does not mean we should be going around grinning all the time! Nor does it mean that we have to have bouncy folk music or boring back-slapping heartiness whenever we meet in the ecclesia. It reflects the deeper joy of knowing that in Christ our sins can be forgiven and that beyond the sufferings and trials of the present is the glory of the Kingdom of God (see Romans 5:1-11). If that is the basis of our happiness, then we shall want to live in harmony with each other, and to find pleasure in the work of the Lord rather than in what passes for entertainment in the world around us.

But at the same time, we _will_ want to express our joy in enthusiastic worship and warmth of fellowship! Remember how Paul and Silas, even after they had been beaten and thrown into prison, "prayed, and sang praises unto God" (Acts 16:25). _There_ was the spirit which enabled them to rejoice in suffering for Christ.

5: **_"moderation"_** = forbearance, considerateness (the same Greek word is translated "gentleness" in 2 Corinthians 10:1). We need consideration for one another if we are to agree. What's more, since we are called on to witness for the Lord to all men, we need to set a good example of the lovingkindness of our Heavenly Father.

The Lord is at Hand

We would think twice about unholy arguments if we remembered that "the Lord is at hand". This has two meanings:

1. The Lord is close to all those who fear him and call upon his name. "Where two or three are gathered together in my name, there am I in the midst of them" (Matthew 18:20). This reassuring verse is also a warning. It comes in the middle of the Lord's teaching about forgiveness and settling differences in a brotherly fashion.

2. The return of the Lord to establish God's kingdom on earth will soon come about. For all who have died in the meantime, their next waking moment will be at that event (see 1:23).

6: **_"Be careful for nothing"_** is misleading. R.S.V. translates: "Have no anxiety about anything". Exactly the same point is made by the Lord in the Sermon on the Mount (Matthew 6:25-34). Worry and anxiety are hard to avoid but they do not achieve anything except ill-health. If we put our trust in God—and above all, if we demonstrate that trust by belief in the Gospel truths and baptism into the name of Jesus—then as members of God's family, we have a marvellous privilege. We can, through Christ, call upon God as our Father. God knows what is best for us. If we lay our problems and worries before Him, then we shall know that whatever happens is for our benefit— though it may be hard to see at the time. "All things work together for good to them that love God" (Romans 8:28); no situation, however black, can "separate us from the love of God, which is in Christ Jesus our Lord" (Romans 8:35-39).

7: That is how peace of mind is achieved. How reassured a small child is when it can hold on to its father's hand when there is danger at hand. The danger remains. But the strength of the father gives confidence and comfort to the child. We must not expect that prayer to God will remove all trials, all suffering, all danger. These things are a part of the present state of affairs in a world struggling under the consequences of sin. God wishes us to learn how to cope with all situations in His strength. It is *in the midst* of the dark storm that the Lord comes across the rough and dangerous waters to calm our fears and lighten our darkness. "Though I walk through the valley of the shadow of death, I will fear no evil: *for thou art with me*" (Psalm 23:4). That is the secret of true happiness, the knowledge that we shall not be left alone in *any* situation, when we keep our hand in the hand of God.

8: Here is an inspiring list of Christ-like qualities. If there is "virtue" (or excellence)—which there most certainlly is!—and if there is anything worthy of praise—of course there is!—then these are the kinds of qualities we should be looking for and cultivating. When we look around at the opportunities which exist in the world for friendships, for recreation, for activity of all kinds, what are the things which are consistent with honesty, with rightness and justice, with purity, with loveliness, with graciousness? We can see that the world would be transformed into an altogether different place if such qualities could be found in people everywhere. The good news is that one day it will be! Are we testing our relationships, our work, our play against these qualities?

9: Paul again reminds them that he has set them an example. His teaching was in word and deed. He had separated himself from worldly pleasures to work for the Lord. We too cannot be friends of the world and friends of God. We must "have no fellowship with the unfruitful works of darkness" (see Ephesians 5:7-13; 2 Corinthians 6:14-18). If we pray earnestly for God's help, then through such guidance as is found in these verses and the knowledge that "I can do all things through Christ which strengtheneth me" (verse 13), we shall be able to avoid the company and activity which will leave us ashamed and degraded, because we will be fully occupied with the things which will leave us truly satisfied and fulfilled. Then we shall realise the meaning of Paul's statement: ***"the God of peace shall be with you."***

Test Yourself

1. What kind of crown was Paul referring to?

2. How should being "in the Lord" help to resolve disputes?

3. What is the real basis of Christian joy?

4. Explain the meaning of "moderation"

5. What is meant by "Be careful for nothing"?

6. How does prayer bring peace of mind?

7. Make a list of things you have spent your time doing during the last week. Now examine them in the light of verse 8. Did they fit into these categories? If not, is there anything you can do about it? What should be the first thing to do?

For answers turn to page 46

I'm delighted that you've thought about me again. Not that I needed your gifts, since I have learnt to accept even the worst situations in the strength which comes from Christ. However, it was good that you wanted to help me, as you did after your conversion when I journeyed on into other parts of Greece. Not that I was seeking help, but I couldn't wish for more than you have provided through Epaphroditus. You will be richly blessed by God through Christ, to whom be glory for ever.

10: The word *"rejoice"* occurs once again as Paul thinks of their generosity. Paul is saying (as in 2:30) that they had lacked further opportunity to make a gift to him, until at last Epaphroditus had been able to journey to him.

"Flourished again" suggests flowers which bloom again each year, a lovely picture appropriate to their kindness. When we show practical kindness to others, we develop lovely and fragrant characters.

11-13: Paul is not rejoicing because of the practical gifts they had sent him to supply his "want" or need. For his joy, as we have previously seen, is based upon the knowledge that Christ has broken man's slavery to sin and opened up the possibility of the kingdom of God on earth. So whether he is being entertained by a rich person, or struggling to survive in a foul dungeon, the apostle rejoices, because he knows this is only a prelude to the kingdom. Read in 2 Corinthians 11: 23-30 the catalogue of sufferings he had endured. In addition he had been afflicted with some physical ailment, which he prayed God would remove. But it remained, and Paul came to realise the great truth:

"My grace is sufficient for thee: for my strength is made perfect in weakness" (2 Corinthians 12:9).

It is when we are up against problems which we cannot solve by human means that we are forced to rely on God. The man out at sea in a sinking ship with no hope of rescue will start to pray. We need to understand that even when the ship of human civilisation may not appear to be sinking, it is. If we happen to be living in comfort and things are going well, it is easy to lose sight of our need for God. Paul knew that the only sure, enduring and eternal happiness was that which came from his relationship with God in Christ and the fellowship which this produced.

"I can do all things through Christ which strengtheneth me": Paul's self-sufficiency is not based upon human ingenuity; it is inspired by the "fellowship of Christ's sufferings". Knowing that Christ managed to live with no significant possessions of his own and "endured the cross, despising the shame", Paul feels the strength coming from a master and companion who understands just what our most difficult experiences are like.

What do we rely on most of all? Our families? Our jobs? Our teachers? Our friends? Our money? Something we possess? None of these of themselves

can last for ever. Only in Christ can we have the hope of lasting security and happiness—for ourselves and our loved ones.

14: *However,* writes Paul, **you did a good thing in ''communicating''** (fellowshipping, giving for the benefit of someone else) **with my affliction,** i.e. helping me in my imprisonment. Fellowship has been discussed in the notes on 1:5,27; 2:1-3. Here the practical outcome of fellowship is emphasised. Their ''communication'' consisted of messages, a messenger and gifts to support Paul's work.

They had contributed to his needs on several occasion:

---

1. When he had first been in Philippi and established the ecclesia (Acts 16).
2. During his stay in Thessalonica (Acts 17:1-13), at least twice
3. On the Second Missionary journey, when Paul was in Corinth (2 Corinthians 11:9).
4. By sending Epaphroditus with a gift to him in Rome (2:25; 3:18)

Paul repeats that he did not *seek* any gifts, but what he sought was evidence of their spiritual progress (''fruit'', see John 15:1-5). He can now assure the Philippians that he has more than enough to meet all his needs, for the things which Epaphroditus has brought were not just practically useful. They cheered Paul most of all because they were a token of the self-sacrifice of the Philippians, evidence that the Gospel message had sunk into their hearts as well as their minds and that

their desire was to contribute to the work of the Lord.

Personal Sacrifice

18: *Their sacrifice* was like a burnt offering. When Noah came out of the ark after the flood, he expressed his gratitude by burnt offerings to the Lord, the smell of which went up into the sky as evidence of man reaching up to God. It was a **''sweet savour''** or smell ('odour'), because it showed a thankful attitude to God, a realisation of God's goodness and man's need of that goodness (Genesis 8:20,21). To burn the animals was genuinely a sacrifice, since they were precious to the owner. The lesson is that we give of our best to God (see Exodus 29:18,25,41; Numbers 15:3). Christ, the best of all men, gave himself completely to the service of his Father and by his perfect sacrifice relieved us of the necessity of making animal sacrifices (see Ephesians 5:2; Hebrews 10:8-10). But we are not relieved of all obligation:

a) We must ''sacrifice'' our lives by declaring our commitment to God's teaching and the person of the Lord Jesus Christ (John 15:10,14; Luke 9:23-26).

b) We must associate ourselves with his perfect sacrifice through baptism (Matthew 3:15; Mark 16:16; Romans 6:1-6).

c) We must go on demonstrating our loyalty to Christ through sacrificing our time, energy and means to his service (John 13:13-17; Hebrews 13:15,16).

19: Paul appreciated that the generosity of the Philippians was indeed a sacrifice, for they were not all wealthy. They had given out of their poverty (2 Corinthians 8:2). **God loves a ''cheerful giver''** and will more than reward those who make real sacrifices in His service (2 Corinthians 9:6-8). The example of the widow who gave her last coin, ''all her living'', to the service of God, shines across the centuries to us today (Mark 12:41-44).

20: Paul acknowledges that the beauty and fragrance of lives in tune with God is a source of praise to God and a reflection of His glory. God's glory is not only in His physical perfection and power, but in the quality of His character, or Name (see Exodus 33:18; 34:8). When God revealed Himself in a Son, the Lord Jesus Christ, that character was seen in all its splendour (John 1:14). In our service to God and His Son (2:9,11), we should be reflecting that glory (4:8; 2 Corinthians 3:18).

Test Yourself

1. Why was Paul rejoicing (verse 10)?
2. Why is he able to be so content?
3. What is meant by ''communicate''?
4. Can you list five occasions when the Philippians made gifts to Paul?
5. Why was their latest gift ''an odour of a sweet smell''?
6. What is God's glory and how do we reflect that glory?
7. What sacrifices of time, energy and means have you made this week for the Lord?

For answers turn to page 47

PAUL SIGNS OFF: 4:21-23

Greetings to all the brethren and sisters in Philippi from all of us here in Rome, especially those who work for the Emperor.

21: *"Salute every saint"*—greetings to every baptized believer (see note on 1:1).

22: *"Caesar's household"* refers to people who were in the service of the Emperor. There were large numbers of people in the emperor's employment, just as today many people work in government service. Possibly they had got to know the Philippians as a result of travelling to Macedonia on official business.

23: Just as Paul began with grace, so he ends with a prayer that the grace of our Lord Jesus Christ should be "with your spirit" (R.V.) or mind. We recall (see note on 1:2) that grace is the giving of God and His Son to meet our needs, a giving which we have not earned or deserved, but is freely offered.

What will please God will be our freely given response: faith in His word (Isaiah 66:2) *and obedience to His will* (John 15:13,14).

Test Yourself

1. Make a list of the things God has provided for us which *Philippians* refers to.

2. What response does God require of us?

For answers turn to page 47

OUTLINE ANSWERS TO QUESTIONS

Some of the questions in the text are straightforward ones, designed to help you test how well you have absorbed the information in the section concerned. Others are more open-ended, designed to help you to think of the personal application of the contents of *Philippians*. So some of the answers which are given below are only guides.

If you can answer most of the questions more or less correctly you are ready to go on to the next section. If you feel you have not done well, it's worth reading through the section again before moving on, looking up the Scriptural passages. Then try assessing yourself again!

A CLOSER LOOK

THE ECCLESIA AT PHILIPPI, PAGES 5-7

1. A Roman colony was like a mini-Rome. Its laws and administration were based on those in Rome. Those living there could have the privileges of Roman citizenship.

2. God told Paul in a vision to leave Asia Minor and go across to Macedonia to preach the Gospel (Acts 16:9,10). Philippi was a Roman colony (Paul was a Roman citizen) and possibly Luke had been born there.

3. Magistrates (Greek *praetors*) and serjeants or police (Greek *lictors*).

4. Lydia met on the sabbath with other women for prayer; she worshipped God; she was keen to listen to Paul's preaching and readily understood the need for baptism into Christ.

5. The men who had been making a living out of the girl who told fortunes brought Paul and Silas before the magistrates, accusing them of causing trouble (they had cured the girl!) and undermining the Roman laws and traditions of Philippi (presumably because they had preached of another king—Jesus, and of another kingdom—the kingdom of God).

6. The jailor assumed that, with the prison doors open, the prisoners would all escape. He preferred to kill himself than face the death sentence from his masters.

7. The jailor had already heard (R.V. makes this more interesting and puts "were listening to") Paul and Silas praying and singing praises (Acts 16:25); probably they had talked about salvation in Jesus as well.

8. Knowledge and understanding of God's Word and belief in its saving message, repentance from sin and the desire to live for Christ.

9. Baptism represents (a) death, because the person wishes to die to the old life of sin by a symbolic burial in water. This burial is linked to the death of Christ, which makes possible the forgiveness of sins; (b) birth, because the person rises out of the water to a new life, just as Christ rose from the dead. Baptism is being "born again" (see John 3:5).

10. Luke stayed in Philippi to build up the newly established ecclesia.

PAUL IN PRISON, PAGES 9,10

1. Paul preached to his guards and to any others who were allowed to come to see him.

2. Paul may face death but thinks he will probably be released (Philippians 1:25,26).

3. The Philippians were keen to show their Christ-like gratitude and love by practical fellowship. They encouraged and supported Paul in his work for the Lord.

4,5. Only you can answer these questions!

CHAPTER ONE

OPENING GREETINGS 1:1-2, PAGES 13,14

1. Timothy was the son of a Jewish mother and Gentile father. He could thus communicate well with both Jews and Gentiles. He had been brought up to know his Bible well and must have shown good spiritual qualities.

2. A saint is any person who, because he is a baptized believer, is sanctified, or counted as righteous, through association with the righteousness of Christ. In other words, although he or she will continue to sin, God will continue to forgive those sins (see 1 John 1:7; 2:2).

3. The Arranging (or Managing) Brethren.

4. Only you can answer!

5. a) grace; b) peace; (Ephesians 2:8,14).

PAUL'S PRAYER FOR THE ECCLESIA, 1:3-11, PAGES 15-17

1. The Philippians have shown a wonderful spirit in their response to the Gospel; they have shown a continuing personal interest in Paul's welfare and his preaching work.

2. a) a common basis of belief; b) a common life in the Lord; c) a practical sacrifice for the work of the Lord.

3. The day of Christ's Second Coming.

4. They had shared the grace Paul was receiving, which gave him strength to cope with his imprisonment and impending trial.

5. Prayer starts with PRAISE to God.

6,7. Only you can answer these questions!

PERSONAL NEWS ABOUT HIS IMPRISONMENT, 1:12-26, PAGES 18-20

1. Paul has been able to preach the Gospel to the soldiers who guarded him and many are discussing it together.

2. Perhaps the only time when we cannot witness for Christ is when we are in the act of committing sin. But even then we could witness by *stopping* our sin and declaring that we are stopping because we have remembered the standards of Christ.

3. Preaching is ''in pretence'' if we are not sincere, seeking personal advantage out of the situation. It is also ''in pretence'', of course, if our message is based on human thinking and not on Bible teaching.

4. a) Return of Christ.

b) Resurrection of those who have been enlightened by the teaching of the Gospel (i.e. they are responsible).

c) Judgement of these people along with those enlightened and alive at return of Jesus.

d) Granting of immortality to faithful, condemnation and destruction for unfaithful.

e) Judgement of nations.

f) Saving of remnant of Israel.

g) Rule of Christ and saints from Jerusalem for 1,000 years, bringing blessing to all nations.

5. Only you can answer!

STAND UP FOR THE TRUTH, 1:27-30, PAGES 21,22

1. "Conversation"—citizenship or manner of life.

2. The faith of the Gospel could be summed up as follows:

a) The Bible is the inspired Word of God.

b) There is ONE God, the Creator, the Father of the Lord Jesus Christ.

c) Jesus was begotten of Mary and of God, by the Holy Spirit; he lived a perfect life and died to save us from sin; he rose again to immortality and ascended to heaven to God; he now acts on behalf of faithful believers and will return again to establish the Kingdom of God on earth

d) The Holy Spirit is the power of God.

e) Man is condemned to death because of sin, but can be saved by belief, repentance and baptism into Jesus, followed by a life of faithful obedience to the commandments of Christ.

f) God has promised that at the return of Christ the resurrection will take place and those judged faithful will receive immortal lives.

g) In faithfulness to His promises to Abraham, Isaac and Jacob, God will finally regather Israel to their land and a remnant will serve Christ in his Kingdom.

h) Christ and the immortal saints will reign from Jerusalem when the Kingdom of God is established, bringing blessing to all nations.

i) Finally God and man will live in complete and eternal harmony.

3. Suffering for Christ brings us closer to Christ ("the fellowship of his sufferings"); to suffer for him is, in a sense, a privilege (just as for some people, to suffer and die for their country is seen as a glorious thing).

CHAPTER TWO
CHRIST IS THE SUPREME EXAMPLE, 2:1-11, PAGES 23-25

1. a) Loyalty to the basis of our faith.

b) a Christ-like spirit of humility: "let each esteem other better than himself".

2. Christ did not grasp at equality with God.

3. By sharing our human life, Jesus was able to be a perfect representative of us, but without sin. In him, therefore, we can be brought to share the perfection of God's life.

4. Jesus was a servant in that he gave himself completely to meet the needs of others.

5. If Jesus is our Lord, we will trust and obey him in all things.

6. You must answer this for yourself!

7. In the Kingdom of God Christ will rule from Jerusalem, assisted by immortal saints and the faithful remnant of Israel. All people will submit to his laws, and worship will be part of the normal pattern of life. As a result there will be peace, security and productive work, using the earth's resources for the benefit of all men. There will be a healthy relationship with nature. Sickness, handicaps and mental problems will disappear and people will live much longer.

WORK OUT YOUR SALVATION, 2:12-18, PAGES 26-27

1. Faith in the Gospel is the basis of salvation; but "faith without works is dead", so we must ensure our faith is not just in our heads, but expressed in our words and deeds.

2. God works in us when we submit to His will (see Isaiah 66:2).

3. Only you can answer this!

4. Paul will rejoice if the Philippian brethren and sisters have held fast to their faith and are granted a place in the Kingdom of God at the return of Jesus.

5. If he dies at the hands of the Romans it will be for his faith in Christ. Thus it will be like a sacrifice, adding to the sacrifices made by the Philippians in their enthusiasm for the Truth.

NEWS ABOUT TIMOTHY AND EPAPHRODITUS AND THEIR PLANS, 2:19-30, PAGES 28,29

1. Timothy had the same outlook as Paul—enthusiasm for the work of the Lord and the welfare of the brethren and sisters.

2. He was worried about the reaction to news of his illness when it reached Philippi. He was worried about the worries of others!

3. Epaphroditus had done what the rest of the ecclesia could not do—he had visited Paul and brought their gift.

4. Only you can answer this!

5. You could find out about them (for example through The Christadelphian and The Bible Missionary) and then pray for their welfare. You could contribute to the various funds which exist to support the work of the brotherhood. You could write to them and encourage them. You could visit them.

CHAPTER THREE

DON'T GIVE WAY TO THE JUDAIZERS, 3:1-11, PAGES 30-32

1. Paul doesn't mind warning them yet again about the dangers of the Judaizers, who wanted to keep the law of Moses.

2. Circumcision reminds that righteousness cannot be achieved by human power but by God's power. It is a rejection of "the flesh", and true circumcision involves rejection of fleshly, sinful human attitudes and practices.

3. "Righteousness of the law" means attempting to achieve God's standard by carrying out all the requirements of the law of Moses—an impossibility!

4. By belief and baptism.

5.

Works of flesh	*Fruit of spirit*
sexual immorality	love
impure thinking	joy
unclean behaviour	peace
false worship	patience
black magic	kindness
quarrelling	goodness
strife	faithfulness
envy	gentleness
bad temper	
self-control	
selfishness	
trouble-making	
creating splinter groups	
drunkenness	
general self-indulgence	

When we consider the fruit of the spirit we see how Jesus showed these to perfection in all aspects of his life.

PAUL'S LIVING FAITH AND HOPE, 3:12-21, PAGES 33,34

1. Seize, take hold of

2. Just as an athlete dedicates himself to training for an event, and then concentrates everything on getting to the finishing tape first, so we must concentrate all our energies on winning the race for eternal life.

3. The calling to share His nature, to be "at one" with Him even as Christ (John 17:21). This will be completed when all the earth is full of God's glory (Numbers 14:21; Habakkuk 2:14).

4. Follow the example of others who live as I do—men like Timothy, Silas and Luke.

5. Immortality will mean reflecting the glory of God in our characters; the fruit of the spirit will be an essential part of our natures and the works of the flesh will no longer be possible, because we shall be sinless.

Because of this sinlessness there will be no more pain, sorrow, ill-health or death. Our mortal bodies will be transformed into the perfection seen in Christ's resurrection.

GETTING YOUR PRIORITIES RIGHT, 4:1-9, PAGES 35-37

1. The crown made of leaves presented to the victor in Greek and Roman games.

2. Disputes should be resolved in a brotherly manner, following the Lord's advice and example of humility.

3. The joy of the believer is in knowing that in Christ sin is forgiven and the future kingdom of God can be a reality.

4. Moderation—forbearance, a considerate attitude, gentleness.

5. Do not be over-anxious about anything.

6. Prayer brings peace of mind because the person who trusts in God and His Word has the assurance that God, as a Father, will not allow us to be tested beyond what we can bear (1 Corinthians 10:13) and will give us the strength and guidance to cope in every situation. "All things work together for good to them that love God" (Romans 8:28).

7. Only you can answer this one!

THANKS FOR SO MUCH PRACTICAL HELP, 4:10-20, PAGES 38-40

1. He rejoiced that they were moved by Christian concern to contribute to his needs.

2. Paul is content because his one and only interest is the Kingdom of God. Nothing else is important to him.

3. "Communicate" here means contribute as an act of practical fellowship.

4. a) In Philippi after their conversion.

   b) when he was in Thessalonica, "once . . .

   c) and again".

   d) when later he was in Corinth.

   e) now he is in Rome.

5. The Philippians were not all wealthy—they had given in many cases out of their poverty. Their giving was thus a real sacrifice, and as an act of kindness inspired by Christ it would give pleasure to God, like the sweet smelling smoke of a burnt offering.

6. God's glory is a) His physical power and splendour (1 Timothy 6:16) and b) His moral perfection (Exodus 34:6,7).

7. Try actually analysing how you spent your time in response to this question.

PAUL SIGNS OFF, 4:12-23, PAGE 41

1. God has provided:

   a) A revelation of Himself and His purpose in the Bible.

   b) The Lord Jesus Christ, the "word made flesh".

   c) The way of forgiveness and hope of eternal life in "the day of Christ".

   d) The means of uniting men and women in a unique and powerful fellowship.

   e) The best influences to develop our characters to produce good and wholesome fruit to His praise.

   f) A vision of the future which gives strength to cope with the present, whatever it might bring.

   g) A living relationship through prayer to sustain and fortify.

   h) Love, joy, peace.

2. God requires us to respond in faith and love by

   a) reading His Word, the Bible.

   b) learning to love and obey His Son, the Lord Jesus Christ.

   c) declaring our allegiance to him through repentance and baptism.

   d) steadfast devotion to "the apostles' doctrine and fellowship, breaking of bread and . . . prayers" (Acts 2:42); and

   e) "patient continuance in well-doing" as we wait for the coming again of Christ.

> **The hope is that you will not only have increased your knowledge and understanding of this part of the Word of God, but that you will feel encouraged, like Paul, to press on "to the mark of the high calling in Christ Jesus".**

MOVING ON

Having achieved reasonable familiarity with *Philippians* and, we hope, grasped the basic meaning of the text, you may like to have a go at some further study.

One of the finest ways to follow up words and ideas in the Bible is to use marginal references and/or a Concordance.

If your Bible does not have marginal references, then be advised. If you wish to take the Word of God seriously (and you must do if you have got this far!) get a Bible with them, preferably an Authorised Version. You can then look up the cross references to other parts of the Bible. Often other passages will help to illuminate the meaning of the one you are studying.

A Concordance is like a dictionary which lists all the occurrences in the Bible of any word you look up. It should also assist you in distinguishing between different words in the Hebrew and Greek (the original languages of the Old and New Testaments). *Young's* Concordance or *Strong's* are the best.

Before you commence any further study, remember to start with a *prayer*. For the object is to get a closer knowledge and understanding of God and His purpose, and to let Him speak to us through His word. Paul sums up why we should study the Bible:

"All scripture is inspired by God and profitable for teaching, for reproof, for correction, and for training in righteousness, that the man of God may be complete, equipped for every good work" (2 Timothy 3:16,17).

Some Possible Assignments

1. Look up "joy" and "rejoice" in a Concordance (or follow up any cross references). Look in particular at the New Testament passages using the same Greek original (or one connected). How many times do they appear in *Philippians* by comparison with other New Testament books?

2. Look up "fellowship" and read the passages listed under the Greek word *koinonia*. Your Concordance may tell you (at the back of Young's, for example) that *koinōnia* is also translated "communication" (1), "communion" (4), "contribution" (1), and "distribution" (1). Using the Concordance now look up these words and write out the passages.

   Try analysing all these uses of *koinōnia*, seeing how the context (i.e. the sense of the passage in which the word occurs) helps you to understand the meaning. What have you now learnt about the range of ideas included in the New Testament term "fellowship".

3. Go through *Philippians* listing as many references as you can find to the following basic doctrines:

   a) God and His Son are one in purpose but separate in identities.

   b) Human nature is sinful (N.B. No reference to a supernatural tempter).

   c) Salvation by grace and faith in the Gospel.

d) Second coming of Christ.

e) Resurrection.

Are there any other doctrines referred to? Note how often Paul urges the Philippians to be united in their faith and to stand by it loyally.

4. Use the marginal references to look up all the Old Testament passages listed. Do they add to our understanding of the words or passages in *Philippians*?

5. What can you learn about prayer from *Philippians*? (Don't forget to include the references to prayer in Acts 16!)

6. What can you learn about Paul's character from *Philippians*?

7. Look up references in the New Testament to Timothy. What do you learn about his qualities and his relationship with Paul?

8. Find out about the background to Paul being in Rome. Read Acts 21-28.

FURTHER READING

The following books are recommended for more detailed study of *Philippians*, and have been particularly helpful to the author of this Study Guide:

Philippians by J. Luke (*Christadelphian Scripture Study Service*).

The Letter to the Philippians by T. J. Barling (*The Christadelphian Office*).

Paul the Apostle by W. H. Boulton (*The Christadelphian Office*).

Also useful and not too difficult: *Paul and his Converts* by F. F. Bruce (available from *The Christadelphian Office*).

A good Bible Atlas helps in the study of most of the books of the Bible (a wide choice is available from *The Christadelphian Office*).

An excellent set of booklets covering basic doctrines is available from *The Christadelphian Office*, along with many other useful aids to study. Write or phone for details.

Whatever you read, make sure it takes you *to* the Bible, not *away* from it!

NOTES